Foundations for Improvisation

Foundations for Improvisation

A Guitarist's Guide to Improvisation

Major Scale Modes with Improv Exercises

Melodic Interval Studies

Neal Harris

N. Harris Music
Rohnert Park, California

© 2018 Neal Harris. All rights reserved under International and Pan-American Copyright Convention.

No portion of this book may be reproduced or used in any form, or by any means, without prior written permission of the publisher:

    N. Harris Music
    nh_music@sonic.net

Cover design © 2018 Neal Harris. All rights reserved.

ISBN 978-1-882857-00-5

Contents

About the Author   vii

Preface and Acknowledgments   ix

1. **Major Scales**   1
    - The C Major Scale   1
    - Flat Key Major Scale Spelling Exercise   2
    - Sharp Key Major Scale Spelling Exercise   3
    - The Circle of 4ths and 5ths   4
    - Flat Key Major Scales (the Circle of 4ths)   5
    - Flat Key Major Scale Spelling Exercise   5
    - Sharp Key Major Scales (the Circle of 5ths)   6
    - Sharp Key Major Scale Spelling Exercise   6
    - Spelling Exercises   7
    - Key Signatures   8
    - Accidentals   8

2. **Intervals**   9
    - Intervals from C   9
    - Interval Exercises   10

3. **Chord Construction**   11
    - Chord Formulas   11
    - The Circle of 3rds and 6ths   12
    - Chord Spelling Exercises   13

4. **Major Scale Diatonic Chords**   14
    - Diatonic Triads   14
    - Diatonic 7th Chords   14
    - Diatonic Chord Exercises   15

5. **Major Scale Interval Exercises in 1st Position**   16
    - Exercises: in 1st Position   16
    - The G Major Scale in 3rds   16
    - The G Major Scale in 4ths   19
    - The G Major Scale in 5ths   22
    - The G Major Scale in 6ths   24
    - The G Major Scale in 7ths   26

6. **The G Major Scale in 1st–5th Positions**   27

7. **12 Major Scales in 1st Position**   29
    - Exercises   33

8. ***The Major Scale Modes***   35
    The Modes of the C Major Scale   35
    The Major Scale Modes from a Common Root   36
    The Major Scale Mode Formulas   37

    Transforming Major Scales into Major Scale Modes
    Using the Modal Formulas   38
    Examples: 38

    The Major Scale Diatonic Chords and Relative Modes   41

9. ***Improv Exercises***   42
    G Ionian   43
    A Dorian   43
    B Phrygian   44
    C Lydian   44
    D Mixolydian   45
    E Aeolian   45
    F♯ Locrian   46

Modulation   47
    Exercises in Changing Keys with Related Modes/Chords   47

Appendix 1
    Interval Exercises in 2nd Position   49
    The G Major Scale in 3rds   49
    The G Major Scale in 4ths   49
    The G Major Scale in 5ths   50
    The G Major Scale in 6ths   50
    12 Major Scales in 2nd Position   51

Appendix 2
    12 Major Scales in 3rd Position   56

Appendix 3
    12 Major Scales in 4th Position   60

Appendix 4
    12 Major Scales in 5th Position   64

About the Author

Neal Harris is a jazz guitarist and composer who has been teaching improvisation and guitar for more than forty years. His studies with guitarists and composers—some of whom have worked with artists such as Miles Davis and Duke Ellington—along with Neal's own unique style and talent have culminated in this innovative guide to music improvisation. Neal continues to teach and perform jazz and original music in the San Francisco Bay Area.

Preface and Acknowledgments

This book is written for the guitarist who is looking for an organized guide to the study of the materials and tools needed for the art of improvisation. The materials are the scales, intervals, chords, and arpeggios used in composition and improvisation.

This is Book I—and with its help, you can explore improvising—starting with major scales and the major scale modes. This is supported by a section on major scale theory in case there is a need to brush up on that.

Next are interval exercises to introduce some serious ways to look at melodically breaking up the scales.

Then comes a thorough workout to learn the major scales in all keys on the guitar. (This section is gone over in every position on the guitar in the appendices.)

Next come the major scale modes explained from multiple perspectives, including modal formulas with an improviser's/composer's viewpoint in mind.

This leads to the modal improvising section with examples of chords that coexist with each mode for you to hear and improvise with, exploring the relationship between them.

Finally, there is a section with examples of some common modulations with related modes for practicing your new skills . . .

To start in this book, you need to have some basic sight-reading and rhythmic skills.

I would first like to thank my students, for whom this book is written and without whom it could not have been. I would like to thank all of my teachers, some of whom are Davis Ramey, Barry Finnerty, Dave Creamer, Allaudin Mathieu, and Will Johnson, and my constant source of inspiration, John Coltrane. Thanks to Pat Harris for her incredible copyediting, and Leland Smith for Score, the music-typesetting software used for all of the music notation in this book.

Major Scales

The major scale is a 7-tone scale. The clearest way to think of a major scale is in terms of intervals because that is how our ear perceives it. The major scale is made up of a series of the two most basic intervals, half steps and whole steps.

>The half step is the measurement of two adjacent notes.
>The whole step is the distance of two half steps.

The order of these in the major scale is:

>A whole step from scale step 1 to 2
>A whole step from 2 to 3
>A half step from 3 to 4
>A whole step from 4 to 5
>A whole step from 5 to 6
>A whole step from 6 to 7
>A half step from 7 to 8

From any starting point, play and sing this series of intervals and you will recognize the result: the most basic scale of all, the major scale.

The C Major Scale

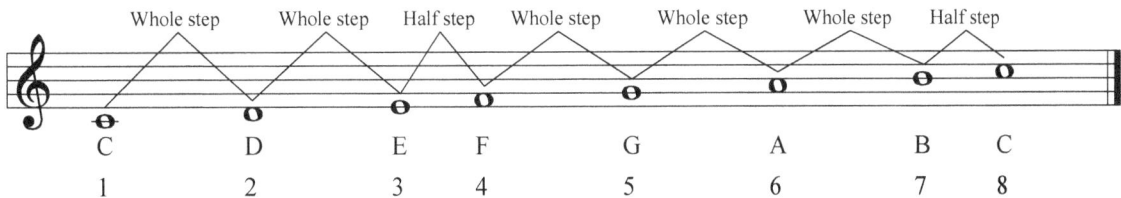

The Western musical system divides the octave into 12 notes evenly separated by half steps. The resulting scale is called the chromatic scale. There are only 7 letter names for the 12 notes. The remaining 5 notes are referred to as sharped (raised in pitch by one half step) or flatted (lowered in pitch by one half step) versions of the seven letter note names. Any note can be lowered one half step by flatting it or can be raised one half step by sharping it. The full chromatic scale (every note) looks like this:

The Chromatic Scale (Notes on the 5th String)

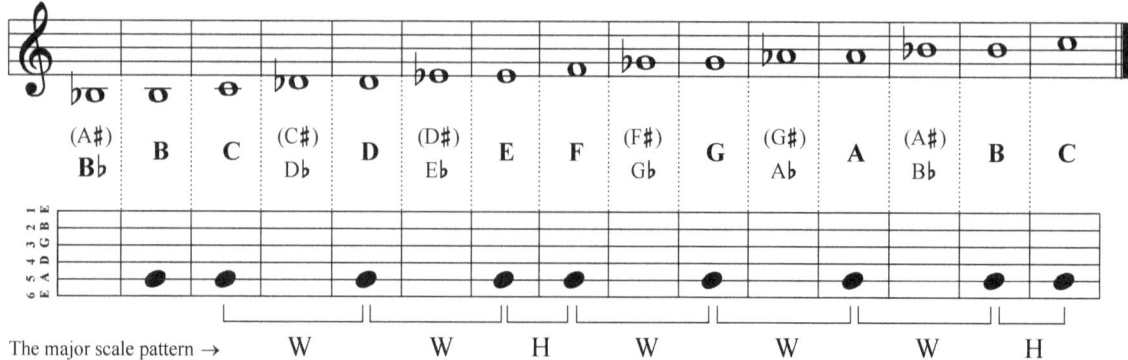

Exercise

From the chromatic scale above, start on any note and write out the major scale pattern (whole, whole, half, whole, whole, whole, half), and notice that from each starting point you will get a different set of flats or sharps (except for the key of C major, which has no flats or sharps). Major scales are spelled with flats or sharps exclusively (one or the other).

Here are two sets of scales for you to complete by adding the necessary flats or sharps to make the correct interval pattern for the major scales.

Flat Key Major Scale Spelling Exercise

Use only flats to complete these major scales. The flat key major scales are spelled out on the bottom of page 5 for reference.

Sharp Key Major Scale Spelling Exercise

Use only sharps to complete these major scales. The sharp key major scales are spelled out on the top of page 7 for reference.

We have to memorize the major scale in all keys. There is an easy way to organize this information using the circle of 4ths and 5ths. The next section explains the circle of 4ths and 5ths and its relationship to the major scales.

The Circle of 4ths and 5ths

The circle of 4ths and 5ths is a 12-step arrangement of 4th intervals as you travel to the left and 5th intervals as you travel to the right. In music, numbers always represent intervals. An interval is the distance from one note to another, measured in terms of scale steps. The circle functions as a chart of key relationships and is useful for spelling major scales. We will first use it to find which notes from each major scale are flatted or sharped.

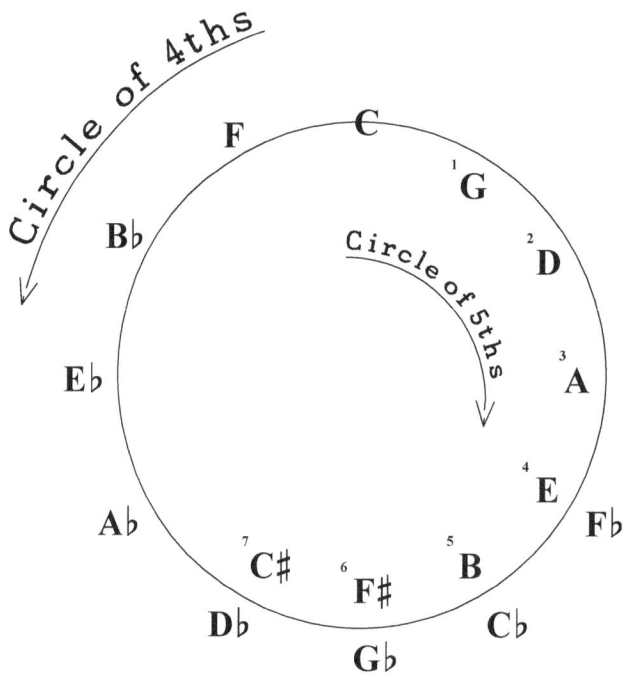

Flat Key Major Scales (the Circle of 4ths)

There are two formulas, one for the flat key major scales and one for the sharp key major scales. First we will work on the flat keys. This formula will tell us which notes (out of the 7 possible) are flatted. The flat keys are represented on the outside of the circle, starting with the key of F major and going around in the 4ths direction to C♭ major.

1. Pick a key (for example, E♭).

2. Always start at B♭ and go (in the 4ths direction) to one 4th past the key you picked. Including all the flat notes you pass along the way, these are the flatted notes in that key. (For E♭, they would be B♭, E♭, and A♭.)

3. Spell the scale, starting at the root and moving in ascending order, and include the flatted notes from the formula (E♭, F, G, A♭, B♭, C, D, E♭).

Flat Key Major Scale Spelling Exercise

1. Memorize the circle of 4ths from C to F♭. (C, F, B♭, E♭, A♭, D♭, G♭, C♭, and F♭.) Note the word "bead" in the middle of the circle of 4ths.

2. Now write out the flat key major scales again, but this time using the circle of 4ths to figure out the flatted notes in each key.

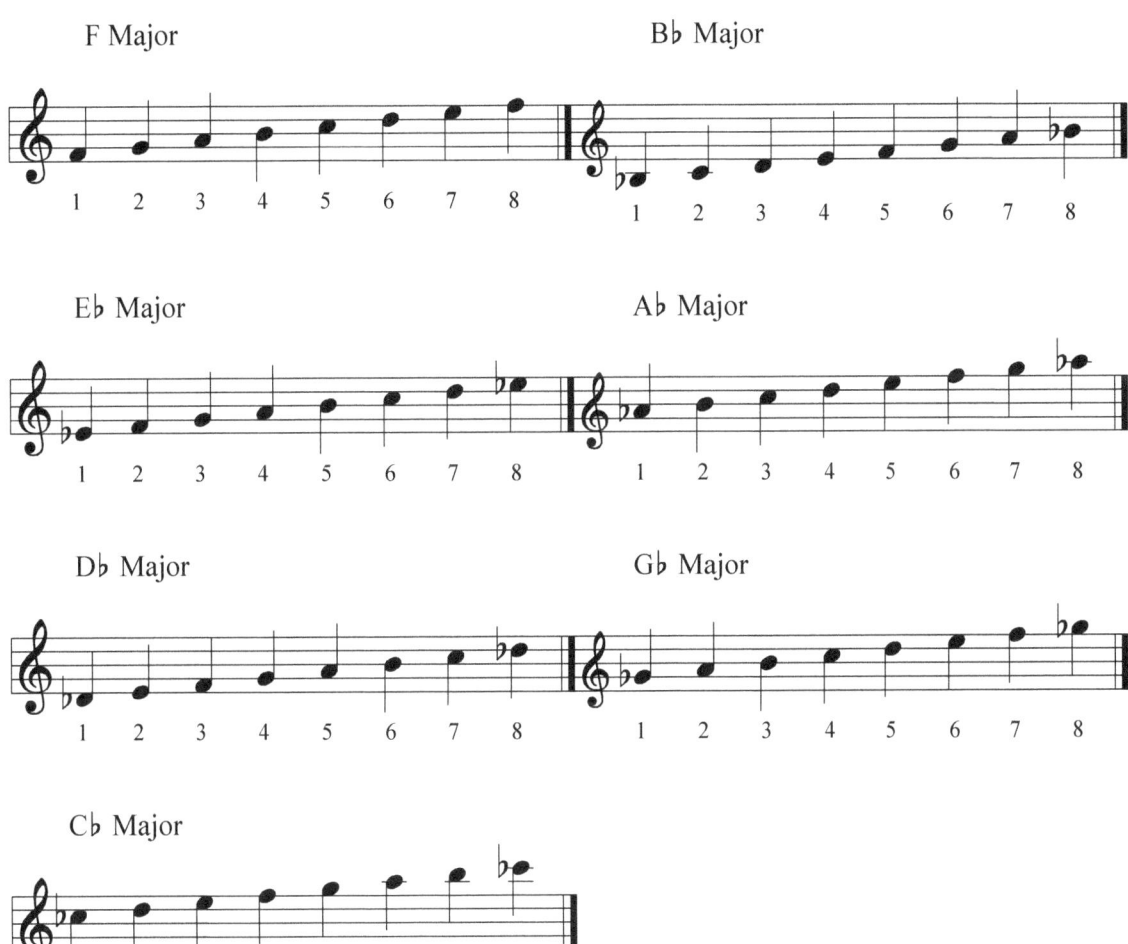

Here are the flat key major scales for reference . . .

F major:	F, G, A, B♭, C, D, E, F
B♭ major:	B♭, C, D, E♭, F, G, A, B♭
E♭ major:	E♭, F, G, A♭, B♭, C, D, E♭
A♭ major:	A♭, B♭, C, D♭, E♭, F, G, A♭
D♭ major:	D♭, E♭, F, G♭, A♭, B♭, C, D♭
G♭ major:	G♭, A♭, B♭, C♭, D♭, E♭, F, G♭
C♭ major:	C♭, D♭, E♭, F♭, G♭, A♭, B♭, C♭

Sharp Key Major Scales (the Circle of 5ths)

For the sharp keys, the number of sharped notes is indicated by the numbers next to each key, starting with G, which has 1 sharp, through the key of C♯, which has 7 sharps. Note that as you go around the circle of 5ths from G, each key has one more sharp.

1. Pick a key (for example, A).

2. Take the number of sharps for the key you picked (A has 3), and for the note names that are sharped, start at F and go in the 5ths direction. (For A major, F, C, and G are all sharped.)

3. Spell the scale, starting at the root and moving in ascending order, and include the sharped notes from the formula (A, B, C♯, D, E, F♯, G♯, A).

Exercises

1. Memorize the circle of 5ths from C to C♯. (C, G, D, A, E, B, F♯, and C♯.)

2. Now write out the sharp key major scales again, but this time using the circle of 5ths to figure out the sharped notes in each key.

The Sharp Key Major Scale Spelling Exercise

Here are the sharp key major scales for reference.

G major: G, A, B, C, D, E, F♯, G
D major: D, E, F♯, G, A, B, C♯, D
A major: A, B, C♯, D, E, F♯, G♯, A
E major: E, F♯, G♯, A, B, C♯, D♯, E
B major: B, C♯, D♯, E, F♯, G♯, A♯, B
F♯ major: F♯, G♯, A♯, B, C♯, D♯, E♯, F♯
C♯ major: C♯, D♯, E♯, F♯, G♯, A♯, B♯, C♯

Spelling Exercises

Practice spelling the major scales in all keys. A great help in learning this material is to spell scales with a metronome. The metronome is an invaluable tool for musicians—so if you don't have one, get one.

1. Assign a pulse at any tempo to represent the notes. At first, you could try two or more beats for each note at a slow tempo.

2. Now spell the major scales in time with the metronome. As you improve, speed up the metronome and use fewer beats for each note. Choose a reasonable task to start! Maybe 4 keys and a slow tempo . . . These have to be memorized, and it is important to learn to break large tasks (like this one) into assimilable small tasks.

3. Keep a record of your progress in terms of specific exercise and beats per minute.

Exercise	Date	Metronome	Date	Metronome	Date	Metronome
_____	__/__/__	_____	__/__/__	_____	__/__/__	_____
_____	__/__/__	_____	__/__/__	_____	__/__/__	_____
_____	__/__/__	_____	__/__/__	_____	__/__/__	_____
_____	__/__/__	_____	__/__/__	_____	__/__/__	_____
_____	__/__/__	_____	__/__/__	_____	__/__/__	_____
_____	__/__/__	_____	__/__/__	_____	__/__/__	_____
_____	__/__/__	_____	__/__/__	_____	__/__/__	_____
_____	__/__/__	_____	__/__/__	_____	__/__/__	_____
_____	__/__/__	_____	__/__/__	_____	__/__/__	_____
_____	__/__/__	_____	__/__/__	_____	__/__/__	_____
_____	__/__/__	_____	__/__/__	_____	__/__/__	_____
_____	__/__/__	_____	__/__/__	_____	__/__/__	_____

Key Signatures

The key signature is a group of flats or sharps arranged on the staff, after the clef sign and before the time signature, representing the primary key center of the music. The key signature affects every note throughout the whole composition, unless:

1. There is an accidental.

2. There is a new key signature.

The flats and sharps are written in the order you get them from the circle (B♭, E♭, A♭, D♭, G♭, C♭, F♭ for flats, and F♯, C♯, G♯, D♯, A♯, E♯, B♯ for sharps).

Each key signature can represent a major scale or its relative minor scale.

Key Signatures in All Keys

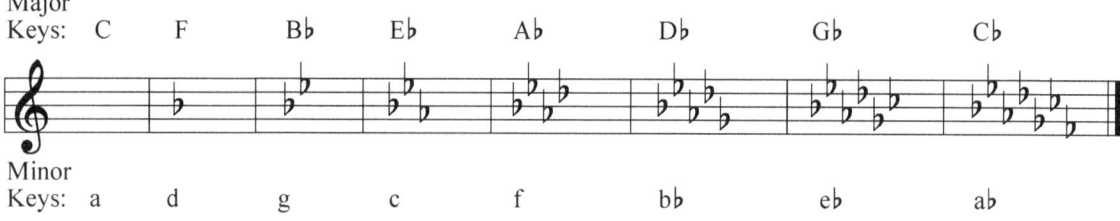

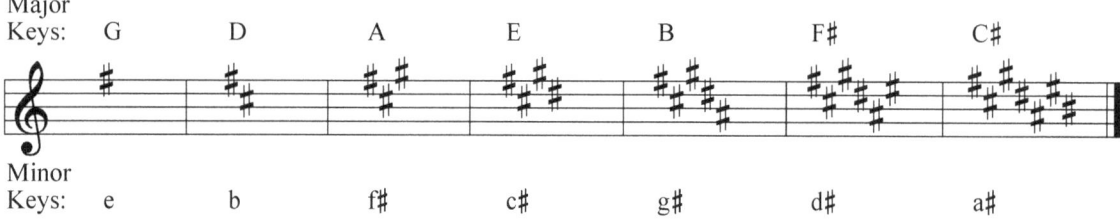

Accidentals

An accidental is a sharp, flat, or natural occurring in the music that temporarily differs from the key signature. The accidental affects only the notes after it, within the same measure and in the same octave. The natural sign returns a note to its unaltered state.

2

Intervals

An interval is the distance of one note to another measured in terms of major scale steps. When analyzing an ascending interval, the lower note becomes the key center and you compare the higher note with the lower note's major scale.

The 2nd, 3rd, 6th, and 7th scale degrees are:

* Major intervals if they match the major scale of the lower note.
* Minor intervals if they are one half step lower.
* Diminished intervals if they are two half steps lower but retain the same note name (for example, B♭♭ in the key of C major is a diminished 7th).
* Augmented intervals if they are one half step higher.

The 4th, 5th, and 8th (octave) scale degrees are:

* Perfect if they match the major scale of the lower note.
* Diminished intervals if they are one half step lower.
* Augmented intervals if they are one half step higher.

Here is a chart of the most common intervals as they relate to C major.

Intervals from C

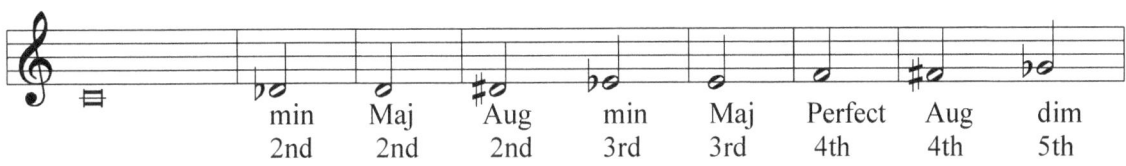

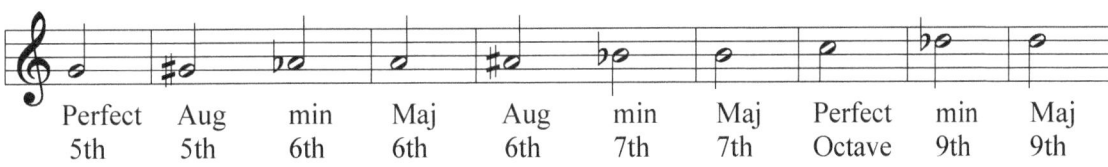

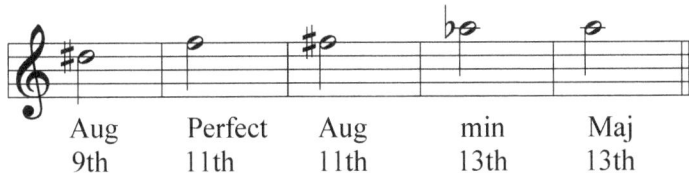

9

Interval Exercises

Practice spelling intervals using the circle of 4ths and 5ths as a way to get through all keys. Take one interval at a time and spell it in each key going around the circle. (The circle is just one way of ensuring that you have covered every key. You could also use the chromatic scale, etc.) Use the metronome, and for each beat, spell the interval you are working on in the next key. Here is a chart to help you keep track of your progress.

Intervals	Date	Metronome	Date	Metronome	Date	Metronome
Major 2nd	___/___/___	_____	___/___/___	_____	___/___/___	_____
Major 3rd	___/___/___	_____	___/___/___	_____	___/___/___	_____
Perfect 4th	___/___/___	_____	___/___/___	_____	___/___/___	_____
Perfect 5th	___/___/___	_____	___/___/___	_____	___/___/___	_____
Major 6th	___/___/___	_____	___/___/___	_____	___/___/___	_____
Major 7th	___/___/___	_____	___/___/___	_____	___/___/___	_____
minor 2nd	___/___/___	_____	___/___/___	_____	___/___/___	_____
minor 3rd	___/___/___	_____	___/___/___	_____	___/___/___	_____
minor 6th	___/___/___	_____	___/___/___	_____	___/___/___	_____
minor 7th	___/___/___	_____	___/___/___	_____	___/___/___	_____
diminished 5th	___/___/___	_____	___/___/___	_____	___/___/___	_____
diminished 7th	___/___/___	_____	___/___/___	_____	___/___/___	_____
Augmented 4th	___/___/___	_____	___/___/___	_____	___/___/___	_____
Augmented 5th	___/___/___	_____	___/___/___	_____	___/___/___	_____
Augmented 6th	___/___/___	_____	___/___/___	_____	___/___/___	_____

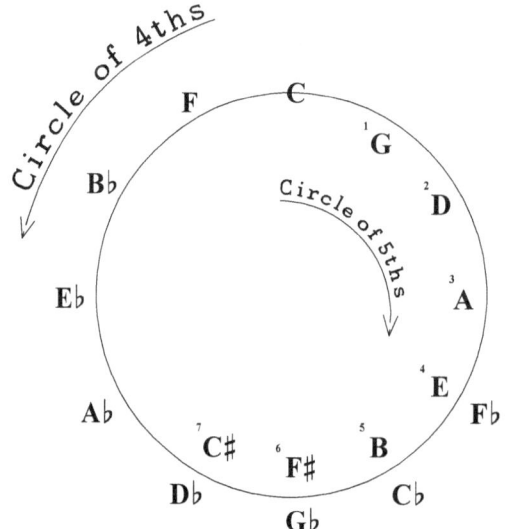

3

Chord Construction

Chords are constructed from scale tones. Now that you can spell major scales in all keys, they are useful as a foundation for a set of formulas (in this case) for different types of chords. Now a simple formula for anything will give you the same result in all keys. Apply the chord formulas below to the major scale with the same root as the chord you want to build.

The C Major Scale

Chord Formulas

Triads

Major (Maj)	= 1, 3, and 5
Minor (min)	= 1, ♭3, and 5
Diminished (°)	= 1, ♭3, and ♭5
Augmented (Aug)	= 1, 3, and ♯5

7th Chords

Major 7 (Δ7) (Maj7)	= 1, 3, 5, 7
Dominant 7 (7)	= 1, 3, 5, ♭7
Minor 7 (–7) (min7)	= 1, ♭3, 5, ♭7
Half Diminished (ø7)	= 1, ♭3, ♭5, ♭7
Diminished (°7)	= 1, ♭3, ♭5, ♭♭7

Notice that these chords are constructed of 3rds (every other note) and that the skipped notes (2, 4, and 6) reappear as "extensions" (9, 11, and 13). This is because they are usually added on top of the 1, 3, 5, 7, so they are labeled as such.

Also notice that the 3rd and 7th tones determine the chord type in the major 7, dominant 7, and minor 7 chord families. Because of this, extensions can be added to major 7, minor 7, and dominant 7 chords without changing chord type (this is also true of major and minor triads). Extensions add color and hues to the above chords, so extensions are often referred to as color tones.

If any other note is needed in a chord voicing, it will be asked for in the chord's label—for example:

C13:	Add the 13th to a C dominant 7 chord.
A–9:	Add the 9th to an A minor 7 chord.
CMaj 9:	Add the 9th to a C major 7 chord.
C7♯9:	Add the ♯9th to a C dominant 7 chord.
D–7♭5:	Flat the 5th of a D minor 7 chord.

11

Memorize the circle of 3rds to help you name 3rd intervals quickly. A triad is 2 3rds (3 notes), and a 7th chord is 3 3rds (4 notes). Superimpose the key signature of the root of the chord, and the formula of any chord you want, over progressions of 3 and 4 notes (starting on the chord's root) from the circle of 3rds to get all the triads and 7th chords. Here are some examples:

Triads

C major	=	C, E, and G
C minor	=	C, E♭, and G
F major	=	F, A, and C
F minor	=	F, A♭, and C
B♭ major	=	B♭, D, and F
B♭ minor	=	B♭, D♭, and F

7th Chords

C Maj 7	=	C, E, G, and B
C7	=	C, E, G, and B♭
C–7	=	C, E♭, G, and B♭
F Maj 7	=	F, A, C, and E
F7	=	F, A, C, and E♭
F–7	=	F, A♭, C, and E♭

The Circle of 3rds and 6ths

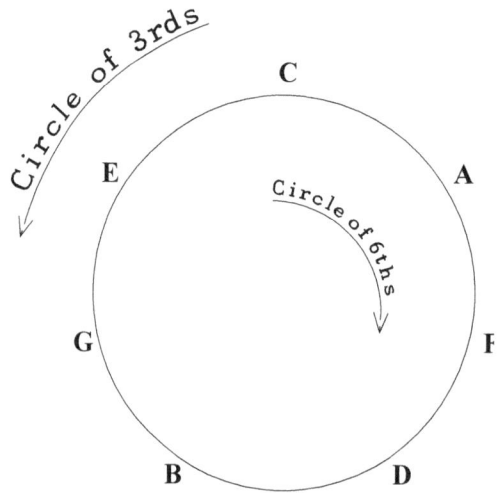

12

Chord Spelling Exercises

Practice spelling each chord in all keys. Start with triads and go on to 7th chords and extended 7th chords. Again, use the circle of 4ths and 5ths as a way to get through all keys. Use the metronome, and spell one note of the chord you are working on for each beat. Here is a chart to help keep track of your progress.

Chord	Date	Metronome	Date	Metronome	Date	Metronome
Triads						
Major	__/__/__	_____	__/__/__	_____	__/__/__	_____
Minor	__/__/__	_____	__/__/__	_____	__/__/__	_____
Diminished	__/__/__	_____	__/__/__	_____	__/__/__	_____
Augmented	__/__/__	_____	__/__/__	_____	__/__/__	_____
7th Chords						
Major 7th	__/__/__	_____	__/__/__	_____	__/__/__	_____
Dominant 7th	__/__/__	_____	__/__/__	_____	__/__/__	_____
Minor 7th	__/__/__	_____	__/__/__	_____	__/__/__	_____
Minor 7th ♭5	__/__/__	_____	__/__/__	_____	__/__/__	_____
Diminished 7th	__/__/__	_____	__/__/__	_____	__/__/__	_____

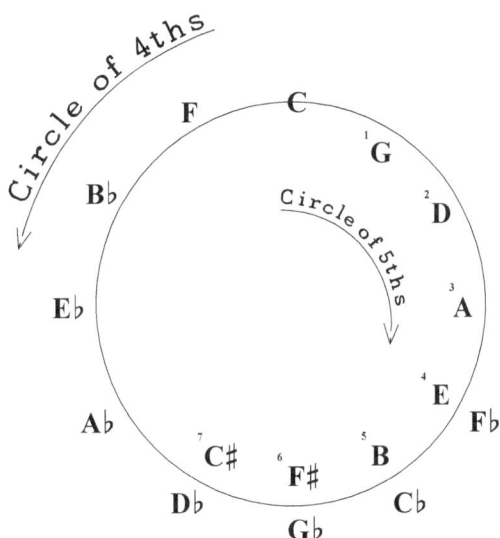

Major Scale Diatonic Chords

Diatonic chords are a set of chords constructed exclusively from the tones of their related scale. Here is an example of the diatonic triads and 7th chords related to the C major scale. Once we define the qualities of each scale tone chord in one major scale, these chord–scale relationships will remain constant with all major scales. (If the IV triad is major in the key of C major, the IV triad of any major scale will be major, etc.)

Diatonic Triads

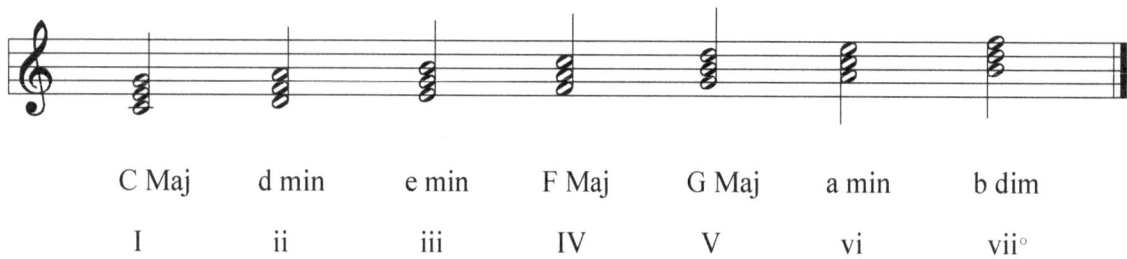

| C Maj | d min | e min | F Maj | G Maj | a min | b dim |
| I | ii | iii | IV | V | vi | vii° |

In any major key . . .

The I, IV, and V triads are major.
The ii, iii, and vi triads are minor.
The vii triad is diminished.

Diatonic 7th Chords

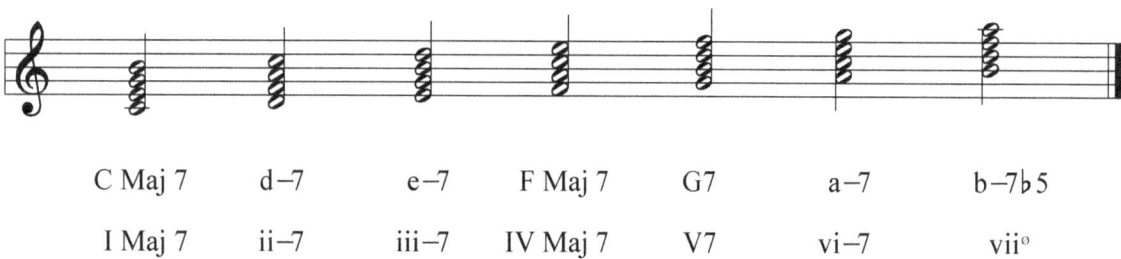

| C Maj 7 | d–7 | e–7 | F Maj 7 | G7 | a–7 | b–7♭5 |
| I Maj 7 | ii–7 | iii–7 | IV Maj 7 | V7 | vi–7 | vii° |

In any major key . . .

The I and IV chords are major 7.
The V chord is dominant 7.
The ii, iii, and vi chords are minor 7.
The vii chord is half diminished.

Diatonic Chord Exercises

Practice naming the diatonic chord families in each key. Start with triads and go on to 7th chords. Here are 2 charts to help you visualize the exercise in all keys.

Triads

I	ii	iii	IV	V	vi	vii°
C						
F						
B♭						
E♭						
A♭						
D♭						
G♭						
C♭						
G						
D						
A						
E						
B						
F♯						
C♯						

7th Chords

I Maj 7	ii –7	iii –7	IV Maj 7	V7	vi –7	vii ⌀
C Maj 7						
F Maj 7						
B♭ Maj 7						
E♭ Maj 7						
A♭ Maj 7						
D♭ Maj 7						
G♭ Maj 7						
C♭ Maj 7						
G Maj 7						
D Maj 7						
A Maj 7						
E Maj 7						
B Maj 7						
F♯ Maj 7						
C♯ Maj 7						

Major Scale Interval Exercises in 1st Position

Here is the G major scale in 1st position on guitar and in music notation. Memorize them and then go on to the following interval exercises.

The G Major Scale in 3rds

Exercise 3

Exercise 4: The Diatonic Major Triad Arpeggios in G Major

Exercise 5

Exercise 6: The Diatonic Major 7th Arpeggios in G Major

Exercise 7

The G Major Scale in 4ths

To play 4th intervals on guitar, we need to use a technique called finger rolling. This is used whenever we are crossing from one string to another on the same fret using the same finger.

1. When ascending, play the first note with the fingertip and lay the finger down in a rolling motion so that when you contact the next string you are letting up on the 1st note. Time this so that as you play the 2nd note you are just deadening the 1st.

2. When descending, start on the flat part of your finger and roll up to the 2nd note so that you end up on your fingertip on the 2nd note.

Exercise 1

Exercise 2

Exercise 3

Exercise 4

Exercise 5

Exercise 6

Exercise 7

Exercise 8

Notice that in this exercise, the note names follow the circle of 4ths but stay diatonic in G major (G, C, F♯, B, E, A, D, G, etc.).

The G Major Scale in 5ths

Exercise 1

Exercise 2

Exercise 3

Exercise 4

Exercise 5

Exercise 6

Exercise 7

Exercise 8

    This exercise mixes 4ths and 5ths. Notice that as it ascends, the note names follow the circle of 5ths but stay diatonic in G major (G, D, A, E, B, F♯, C, G, etc.). As the exercise descends, the note names follow the circle of 4ths (A, D, G, C, F♯, B, E, A, etc.).

The G Major Scale in 6ths

Exercise 1

Exercise 2

Exercise 3

Exercise 4

Notice that as this exercise ascends, the note names follow the circle of 6ths, staying diatonic in G major (G, E, C, A, F♯, D, B, G, etc.). As the exercise descends, the note names follow the circle of 3rds (A, C, E, G, B, D, F♯, A, etc.).

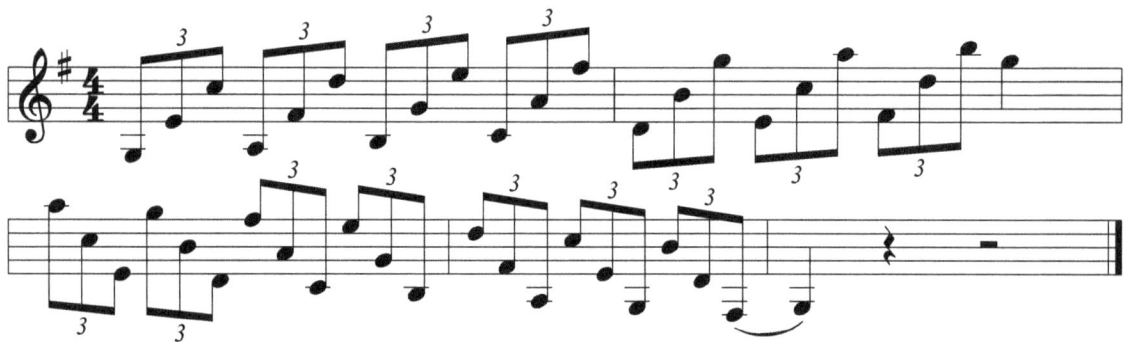

Exercise 5

Exercise 6

Exercise 7

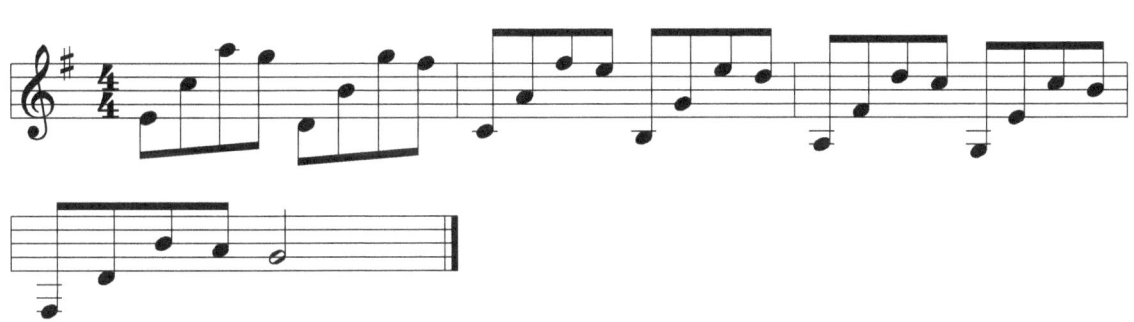

Exercise 8

The G Major Scale in 7ths

Exercise 1

Exercise 2

The G Major Scale in 1st–5th Positions

On guitar, to play the same major scale anywhere, I divide the fret board into 5 positions. (The 1st position was introduced on page 16.) A position is basically a 4 to 6 fret area that is easy to reach in terms of fingering. (Usually assign one finger per fret.) Each position has at least 1 pattern. We will start by memorizing these patterns. (No single set of fingerings will get you through every possible melodic variation, but these 5 fingerings with alternates are a good start.)

The goal here is to memorize these basic patterns for fingering a major scale. These fingerings will be used in many different ways . . . To "see" the notes everywhere on the neck is also a necessary goal, so play the scales slowly at first, pairing the note names with the touch and visual connection.

Work toward playing these scale patterns evenly, practicing with a metronome. With your fretting hand, keep your fingers arched, use the tips of your fingers, and keep your thumb below the top of the neck.

1st Position

2nd Position

 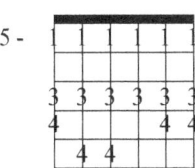  

3rd Position

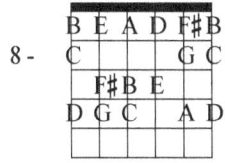 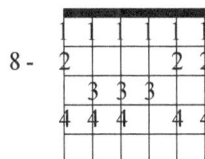

4th Position

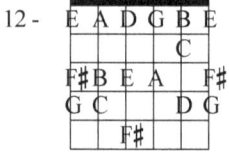

5th Position

7

12 Major Scales in 1st Position

The improvising player needs to have every scale available everywhere, at all times. Let us start with the concept that the same group of notes (for example, low F♯ to A above the staff, as in the illustration below) can be any major scale simply by changing the key signature. After all, there are only 7 note names, and it is the sharps or flats that differentiate one major scale from the next. The goal is to have as full a range of notes as possible within one hand position, so we are not worried at this point about starting on the root. *It is important to hear the root as the tonal center*, but not important that it is always the lowest note . . . Improvising means spontaneously creating melody, and melodies would indeed be boring and predictable if they always started on the root.

The following exercise takes you through the major scales in 1st position, in all keys. With each key, be able to sing the root as you play. Practice these slowly at first, focusing on visualizing the note names on the neck as you play.

Exercises

In 1st position (no open strings), play the G major scale and focus on seeing the neck as you play. Use this scale as a baseline to be able to change to other keys.

1. Start with a major scale that is close to the key of G on the circle of 4ths and 5ths.

2. Spell the new scale.

3. Start with low G or as close as the new scale allows, and go up the scale, flatting or sharping the needed notes as you go.

4. Continue this process, step by step, until you have completed every key.

C Major (from G)

G A B C D E F G A B C D E F G A

F Major

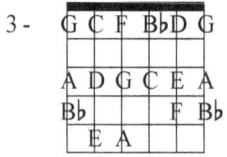 

B♭ Major

E♭ Major

A♭ Major

D♭ Major

G♭ Major

F♯ Major

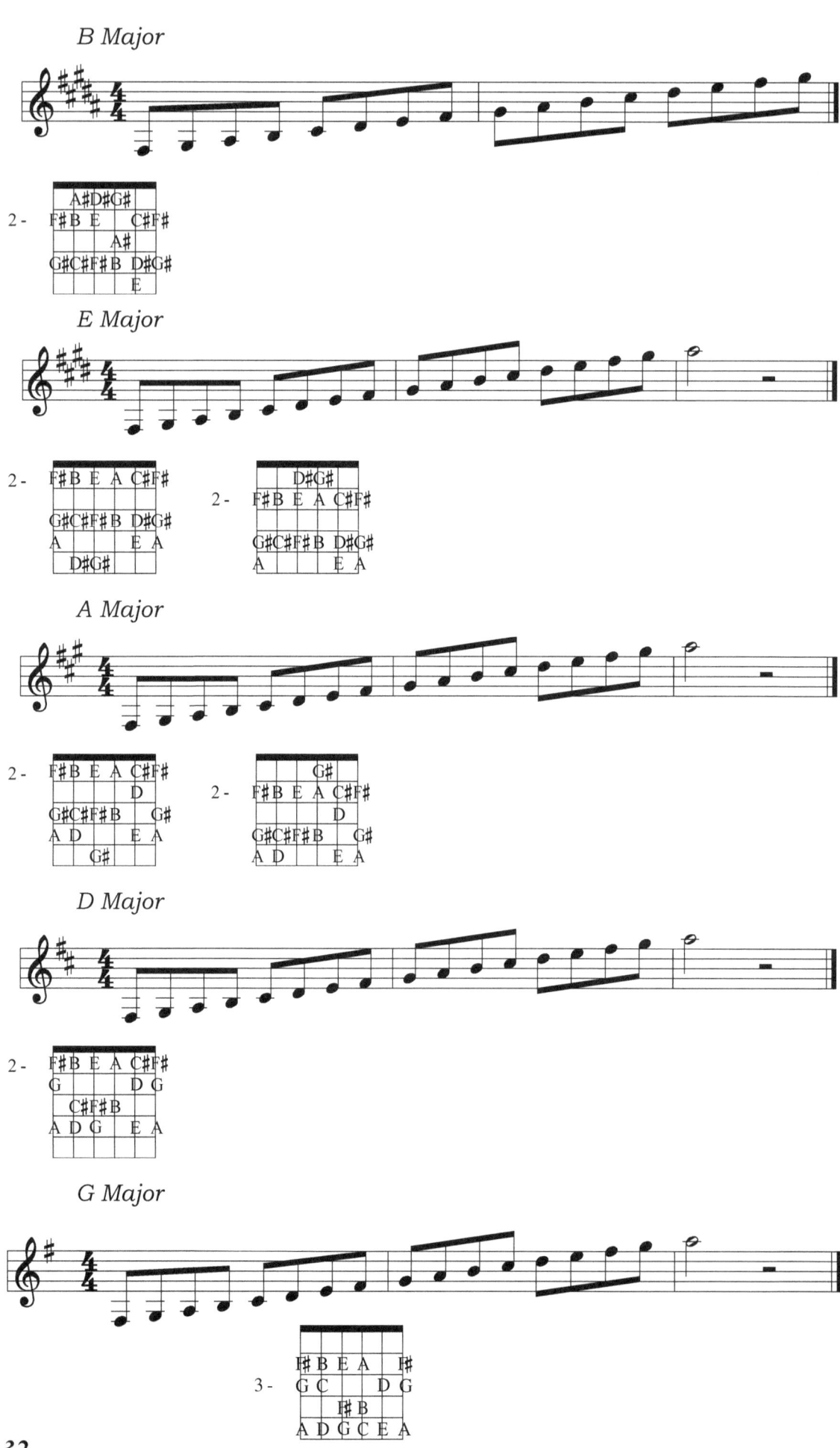

Exercise 1

Now play through these 2-octave major scales in all keys, up one and down the next. Focus on thinking the note names in each scale and visualizing them on the neck as you play. Note the string number notation under each stave.

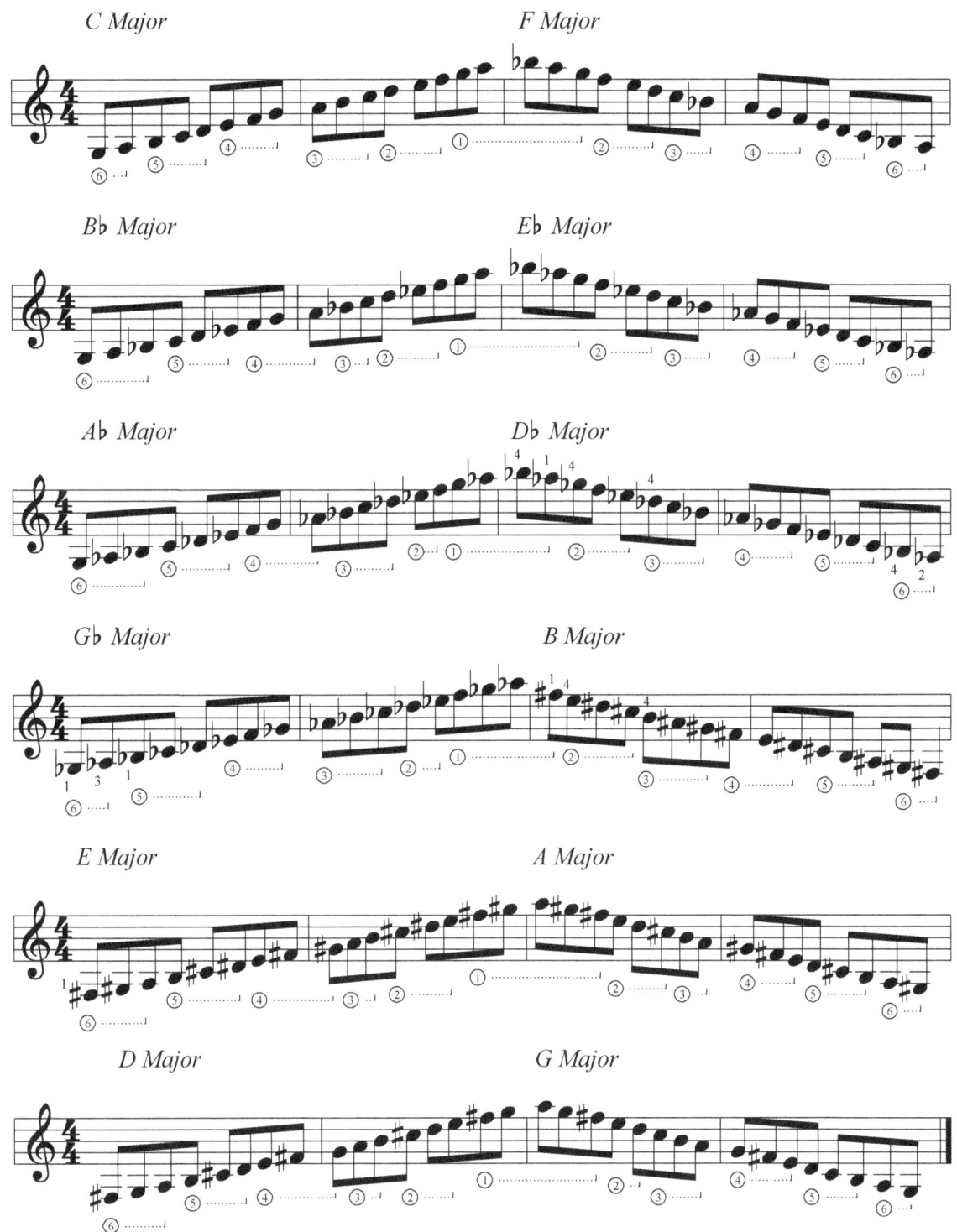

Exercise 2

Here is the one-octave-per-key version . . . For real-life playing situations, we need to know more than just 1st position scales. This example uses the 2nd position G♭ major scale. The 2nd through 5th positions of the 12 major scale fingerings are available for study and reference in the appendixes of this book.

8

The Major Scale Modes

The major scale modes are a set of 7 scales, all derived from the major scale. Each mode has a different tone of the major scale as its root.

* The Ionian mode's root is the 1st scale degree.
* The Dorian mode's root is the 2nd scale degree.
* The Phrygian mode's root is the 3rd scale degree.
* The Lydian mode's root is the 4th scale degree.
* The Mixolydian mode's root is the 5th scale degree.
* The Aeolian mode's root is the 6th scale degree.
* The Locrian mode's root is the 7th scale degree.

Each major scale produces the same relative set of 7 modes. Here are the modes related to the key of C major.

The Modes of the C Major Scale

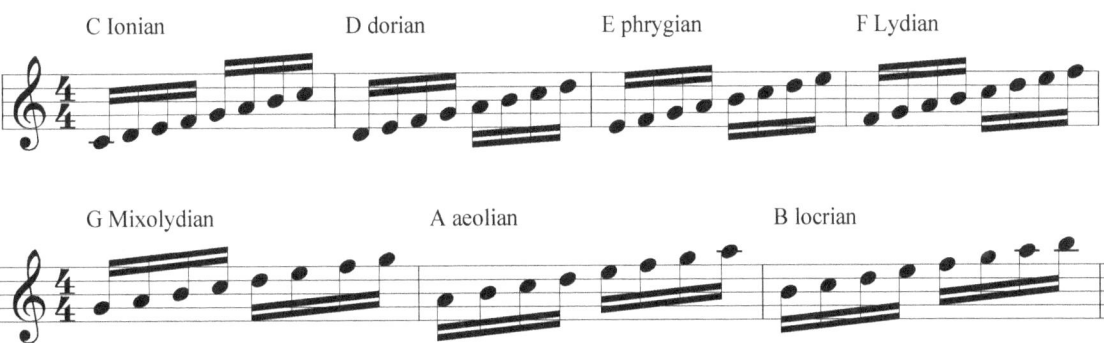

Even though the modes related to a common major scale all share the same notes, each mode sounds completely different. The reason is this: The root represents your ear's tonal point of reference (the tonal center) in relation to the scale. Each mode presents a unique set of intervals above its root and that is what your ear perceives. For example, play the C major scale from A, and focus on the A as root. You can strengthen this effect by playing an a minor or an A–7th chord before playing this scale. This is the A Aeolian mode, one of the minor modes of the C major scale.

Here is an example in 1st position using an A–9 chord.

The A Aeolian Mode

Because each mode has its own unique tonal color, each is useful in its own way. Here are some worksheets of the notes of the C major scale and related modes on the standard tuned guitar up to the 12th fret.

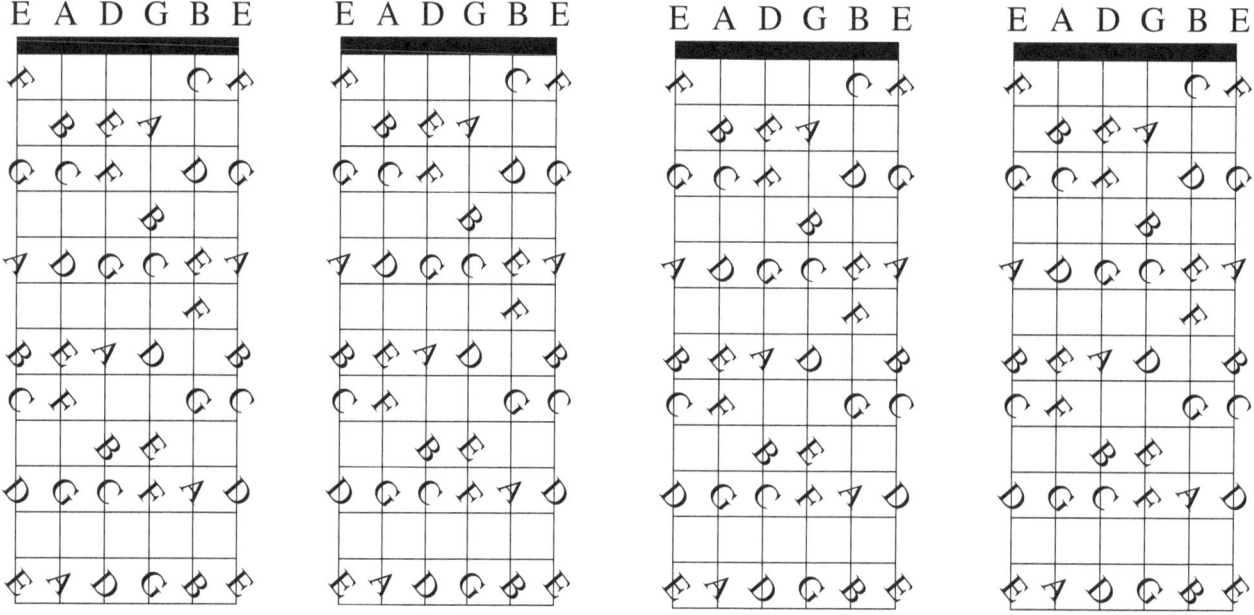

Now it is important to look at the major scale modes all from the same root. It is great to use C as the common root here, because any variance from the C major scale will show up as flats or sharps. We will make a set of formulas from these that can be applied to any major scale to get the desired result.

The Major Scale Modes from a Common Root

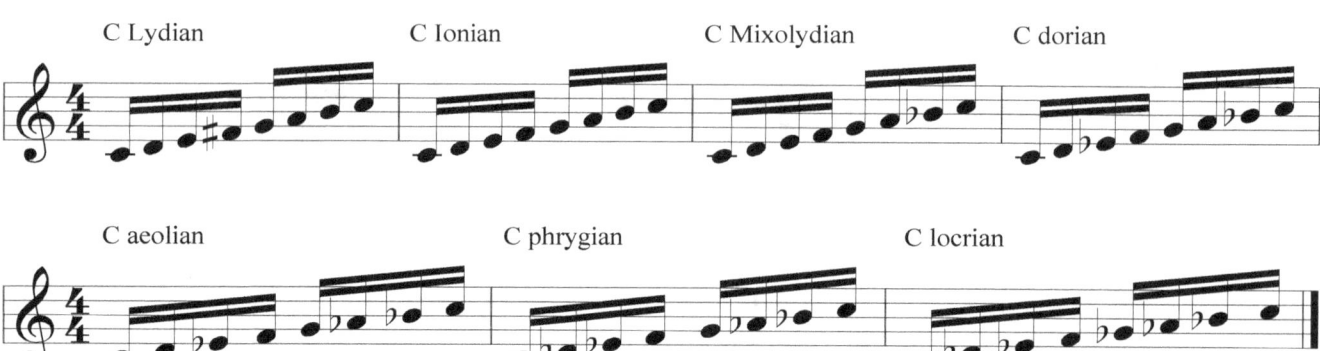

The Major Scale Mode Formulas:

Number the tones of each of the C modes and list the differences from C major as a formula. Here is what you get:

* Lydian = ♯4th scale degree
* Ionian = major scale
* Mixolydian = ♭7th scale degree
* Dorian = ♭3rd and ♭7th scale degrees
* Aeolian = ♭3rd, ♭6th, and ♭7th scale degrees
* Phrygian = ♭2nd, ♭3rd, ♭6th, and ♭7th scale degrees
* Locrian = ♭2nd, ♭3rd, ♭5th, ♭6th, and ♭7th scale degrees

Apply the major scale mode formulas above to a major scale in any key to produce the mode on that root.

Transforming Major Scales into Major Scale Modes Using the Modal Formulas

Examples:

1. G Dorian from G Major

The G Major Scale

← *Fingering*

Dorian from major = lower the 3rd and 7th scale degrees of the major scale one half step.

Transforming G major to G Dorian (the 3rd and 7th scale degrees of G major are B and F♯): B is lowered to B♭ and F♯ is lowered to F.

The G Dorian Mode

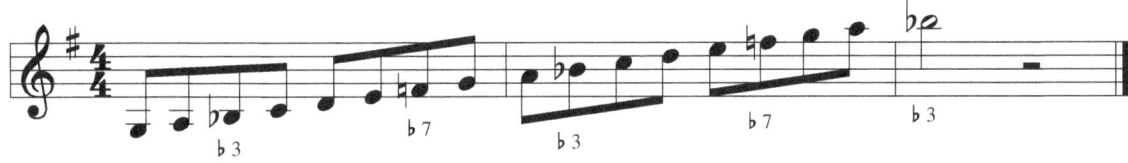

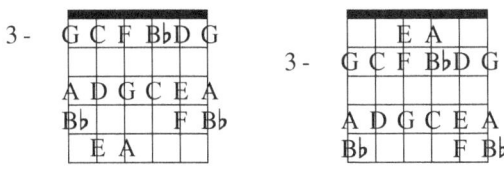

2. B♭ Phrygian from B♭ Major

The B♭ Major Scale

Phrygian from major = flat the 2nd, 3rd, 6th, and 7th scale degrees of the major scale.

Transforming B♭ major to B♭ Phrygian (the 2nd, 3rd, 6th, and 7th scale degrees of B♭ major are C, D, G, and A): C is lowered to C♭, D is lowered to D♭, G is lowered to G♭, and A is lowered to A♭.

The B♭ Phrygian Mode

3. G♭ Lydian from G♭ Major

The G♭ Major Scale

38

Lydian from major = raise the 4th scale degree one half step.

Transforming G♭ major to G♭ Lydian (the 4th scale degree of G♭ major is C♭): C♭ is raised to C.

The G♭ Lydian Mode

4. A Mixolydian from A Major

The A Major Scale

Mixolydian from major = lower the 7th scale degree one half step.

Transforming A major to A Mixolydian (the 7th scale degree of A major is G♯): G♯ is lowered to G.

The A Mixolydian Mode

5. C Aeolian from C Major

The C Major Scale

Aeolian from major = lower the 3rd, 6th, and 7th scale degrees one half step.

Transforming C major to C Aeolian (the 3rd scale degree is E, the 6th is A, and the 7th is B): E is lowered to E♭, A is lowered to A♭, and B is lowered to B♭.

The C Aeolian Mode

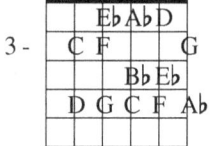

6. D Locrian from D Major

The D Major Scale

Locrian from major = lower the 2nd, 3rd, 5th, 6th, and 7th scale degrees one half step.

Transforming D major to D Locrian (the 2nd, 3rd, 5th, 6th, and 7th scale degrees of D major are E, F♯, A, B, and C♯): E is lowered to E♭, F♯ is lowered to F, A is lowered to A♭, B is lowered to B♭, and C♯ is lowered to C.

The D Locrian Mode

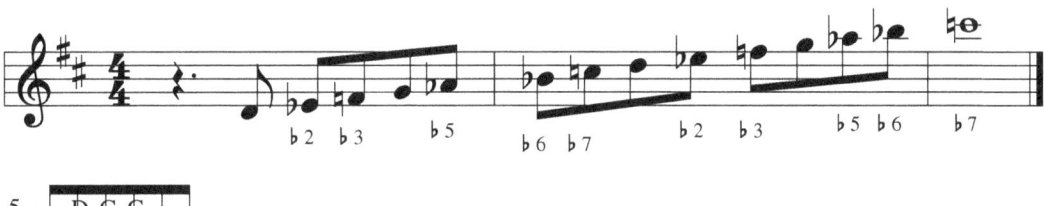

The Major Scale Diatonic 7th Chords and Their Relative Modes

The major scale modes are a melodic expression of the diatonic chord series; the major scale diatonic chords are a harmonic expression of the modes. Here they both are again to help you see the connection.

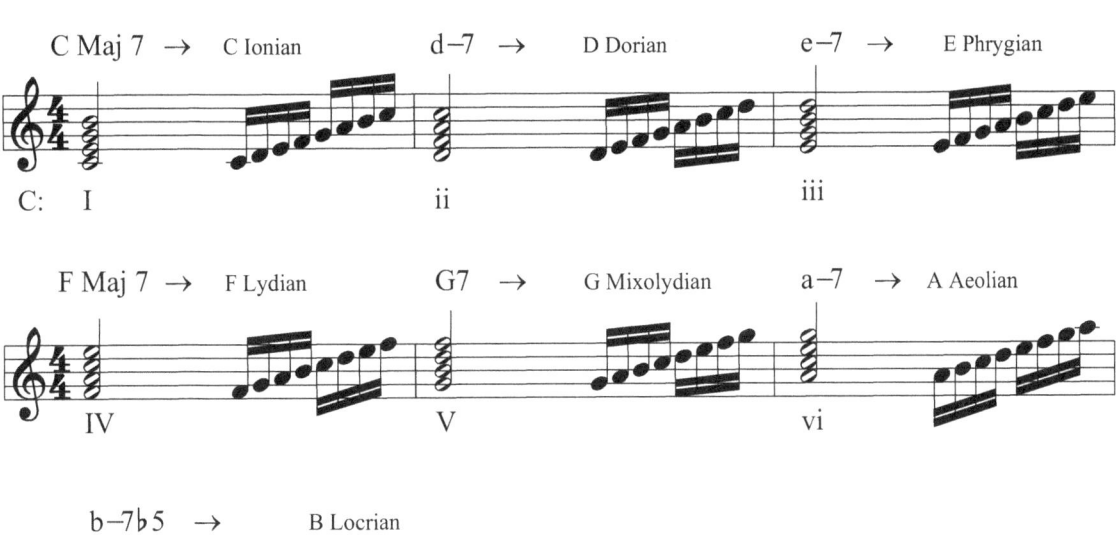

Exercise

Practice spelling each mode in all keys. Take one at a time and use a metronome (as in the first spelling exercises) to cover all the keys. Remember that these are major scale modes and that any one of these modes, in any key, contains the same notes as its related "relative major" scale. That means that after learning the major scales in all keys, you have already played these modes in all keys without focusing on the modal identity of each mode. So . . . the fingerings are the same, but we have to learn to hear each one.

9

Improv Exercises

This chapter combines each major scale mode with some relative chords, an analysis of how to use them, and a set of improv exercises. Apply these exercises to each of the following mode and chord combinations. The following set of modes are all relative to the key of G major, to help make the material accessible and to connect with all the earlier interval exercises. The hope is that once you experience the beauty of these modal colors for yourself, you will be inspired to transpose this material to all keys—and to start composing and improvising with all of the major scale modes.

Exercise 1

1. Warm up—play the mode and the chords you will be using. Play a few melodic patterns to get the scale in your ear and under your fingers. Record or loop a comping pattern using the chords listed for the appropriate mode, and practice playing scale lines over the chords you have recorded.

2. Sing the scale while playing the chords.

3. Go slowly at first and try to create melodic lines in your mind and bring them out on the guitar.

4. Review some of the interval and scale exercises from earlier chapters, transpose them to the mode you are working on, and use parts of the patterns and scale fragments to help you get started.

Exercise 2

Compose a nice rhythmic part for the first two (or 4 or 8, etc.) bars using the following voicings, record or loop them, play them back, and improvise over them. Practice switching back and forth (comping and soloing) in time with a metronome, and vary the tempos. Feel free to vary the phrase length of the example below . . .

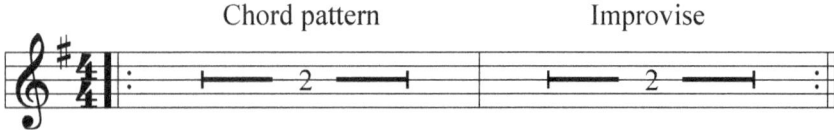

Exercise 3

Practice improvising in each mode with no comping, and at any time be able to stop and sing the root!

G Ionian

The Ionian mode is used for:

1. Unaltered major chords in a major key that are the main or at least the temporary key center.

2. Unaltered major chords in a minor key that are the ♭III chord of that key—for example, the G major chord in the key of e minor (e natural minor).

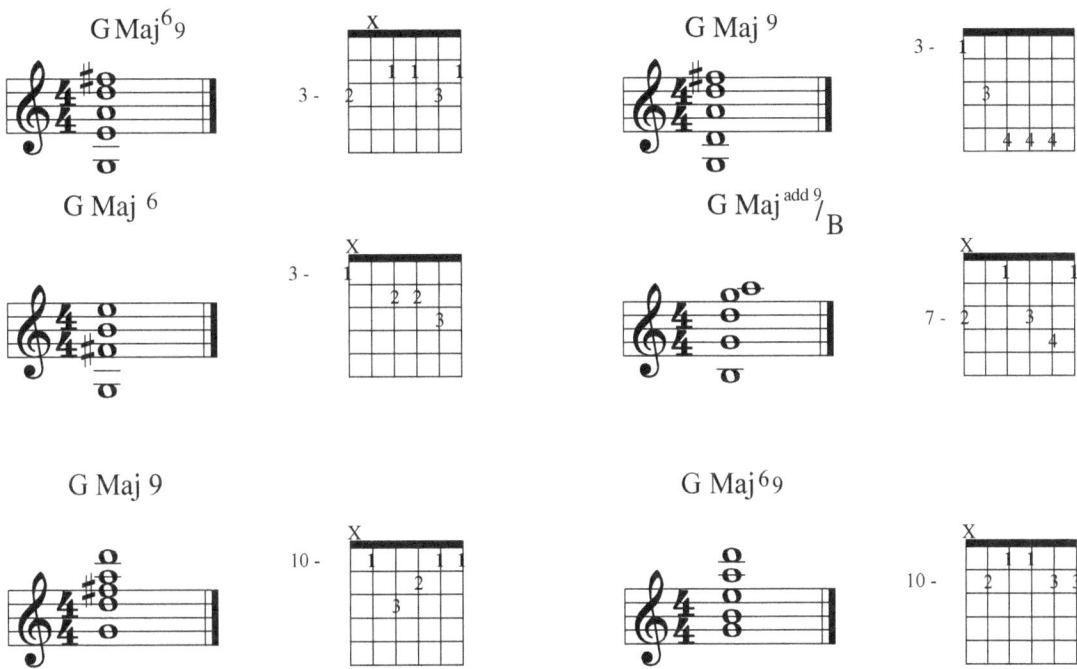

A Dorian

The Dorian mode is used for:

1. Unaltered minor chords functioning as the ii chord in a major key—for example, a minor in the key of G major.

2. Minor chords functioning as the i chord in a minor key. This is only one of many scales that can work in this situation.

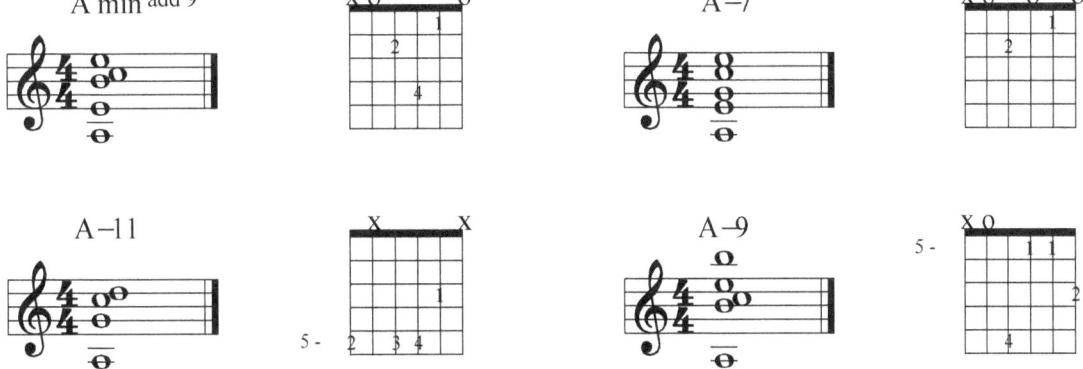

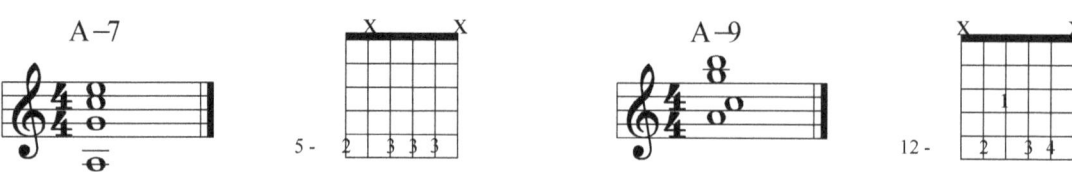

B Phrygian

The Phrygian mode is used for:
1. Unaltered minor chords functioning as the iii chord in a major key—for example, B minor in the key of G major.

2. Phrygian voicings—for example, C/B, CMaj7/B, and CMaj♯11/B.

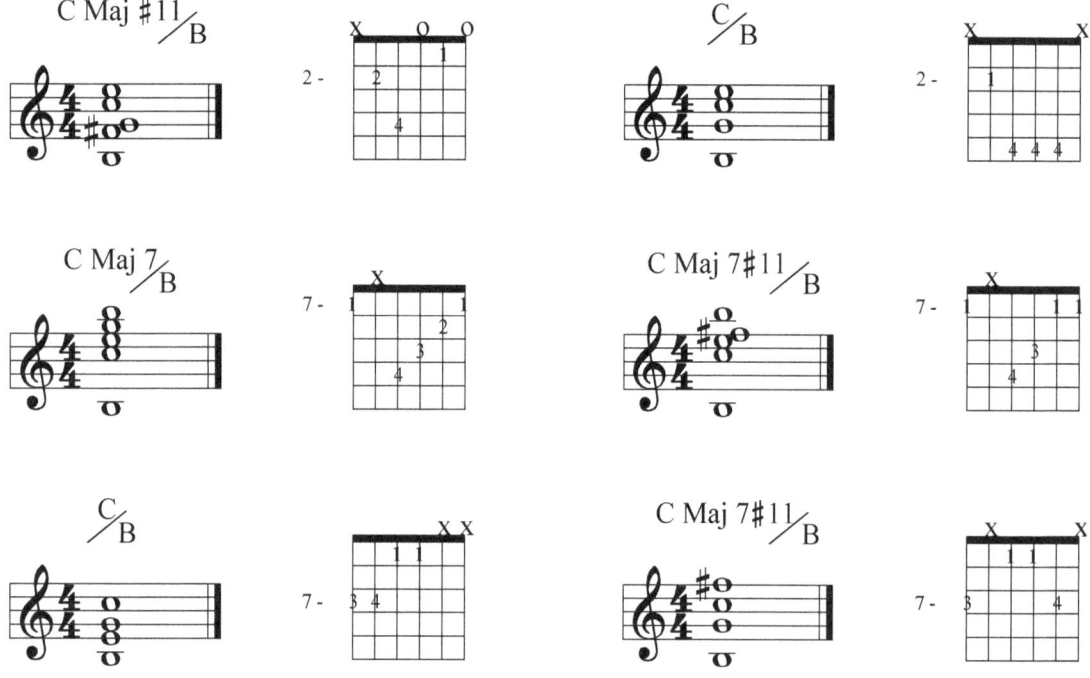

C Lydian

The Lydian mode is used for:

1. Major chords functioning as the IV chord in a major key—for example, a CMaj7 chord in the key of G major.
2. Major chords with a ♯11 (♯4) scale degree in the chord—for example, D/C or CMaj7♯11.

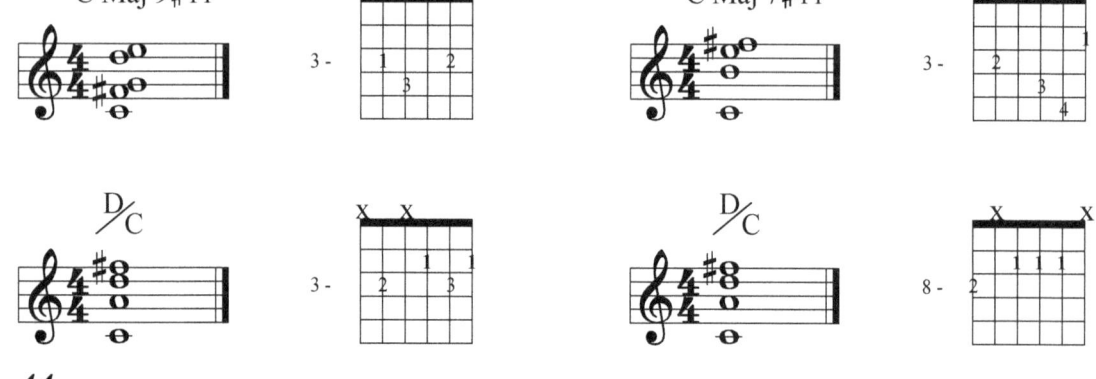

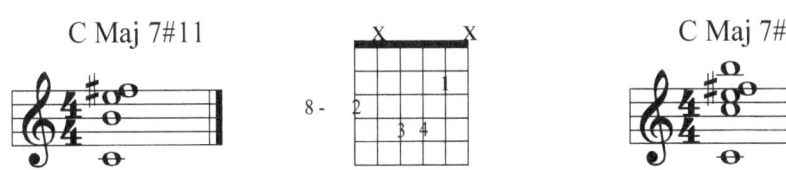
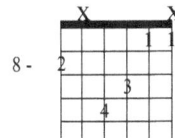

D Mixolydian

The Mixolydian mode is used for:

1. Unaltered dominant chords functioning as the V chord in a major key—for example, D dominant chords (D7, D7sus, D9, and D13) in the key of G major.

2. Unaltered dominant chords functioning as the I chord. A common case where this happens is in blues when the first chord is dominant.

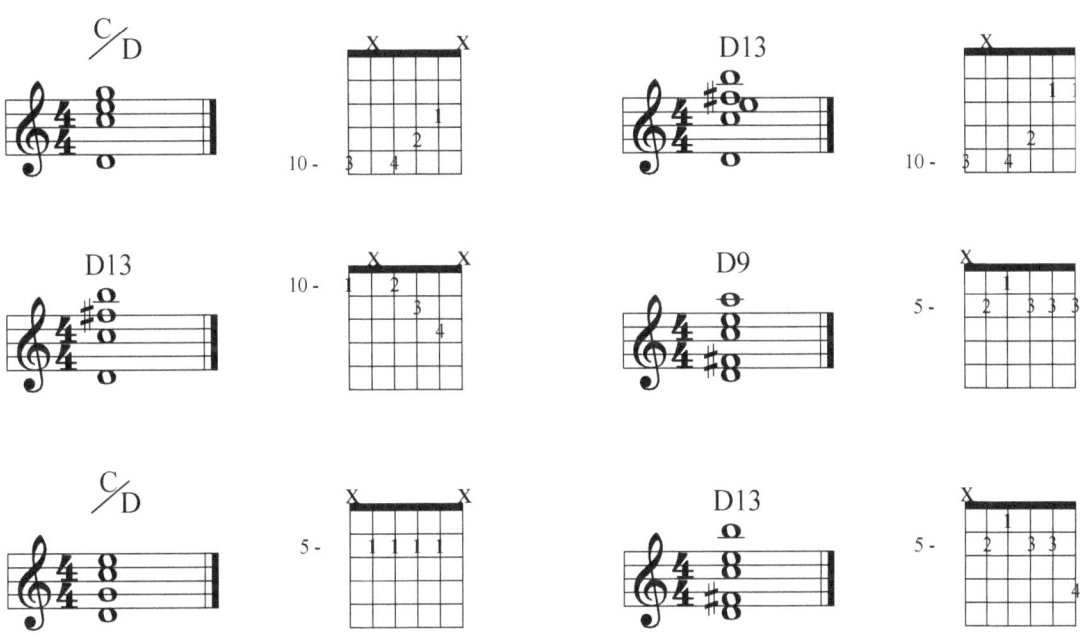

E Aeolian

The Aeolian mode is used for:

1. Minor chords functioning as the vi chord in a major key—for example, E minor chords (E–7, E–7♭13, E–9, and E–11) in the key of G major.

2. Minor chords functioning as the i chord in a minor key. This is only one of many minor scales that can work in this situation.

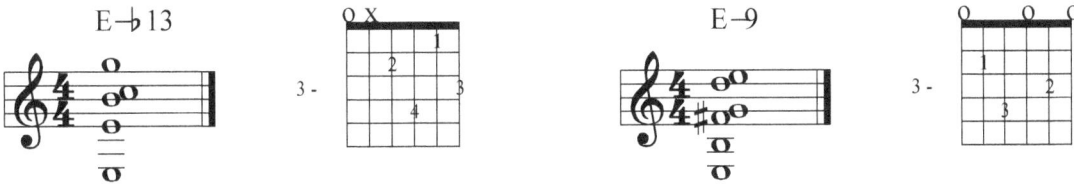

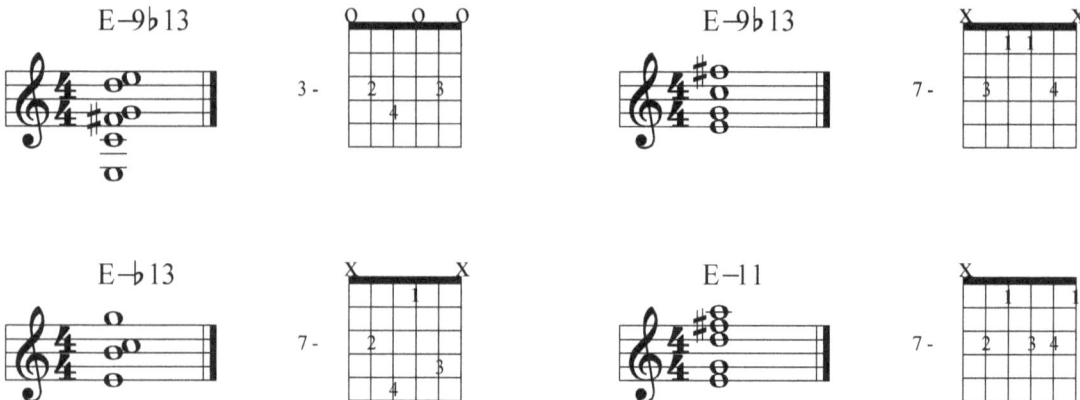

F♯ Locrian

The Locrian mode is used for:

1. Half diminished (–7♭5) chords functioning as the vii chord in a major key—for example, F♯–7♭5 in the key of G major.
2. –7♭5 chords functioning as the ii chord in a minor key.

Exercise 4

Now that you have worked with each individual mode, try composing some chord progressions, mixing chords from any of the diatonically related modal groups. The possibilities are endless. When you find a progression you are happy with, record or loop it and practice improvising over it. As you improvise, try to focus on the mode–chord connection for each chord and the mode's unique quality as it relates to each chord going by.

Modulation

Exercises in changing keys with related modes/chords

Here are a few exercises to practice improvising through a modulation. I have chosen some commonly used modulations (because they sound great) that you will find in many songs.

The I and IV Chords in a Dominant Blues

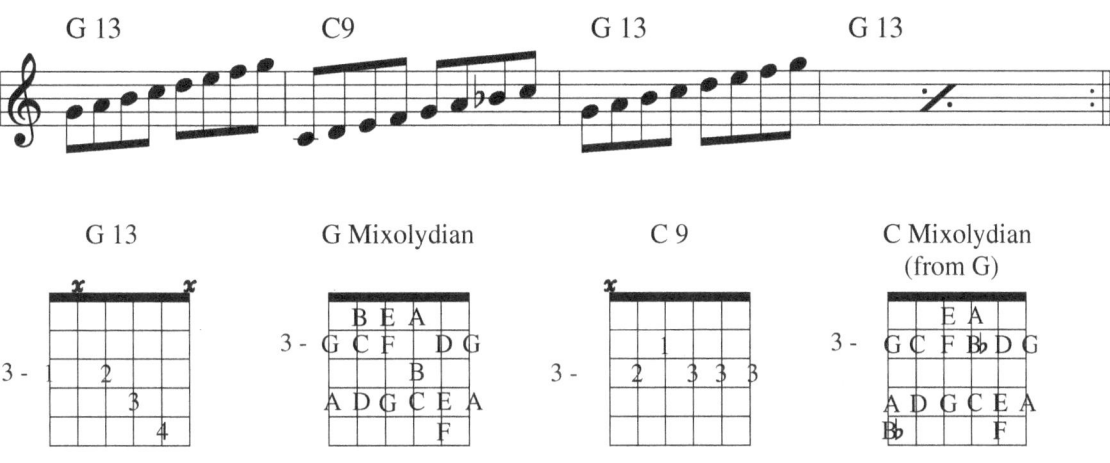

Parallel Major/Minor

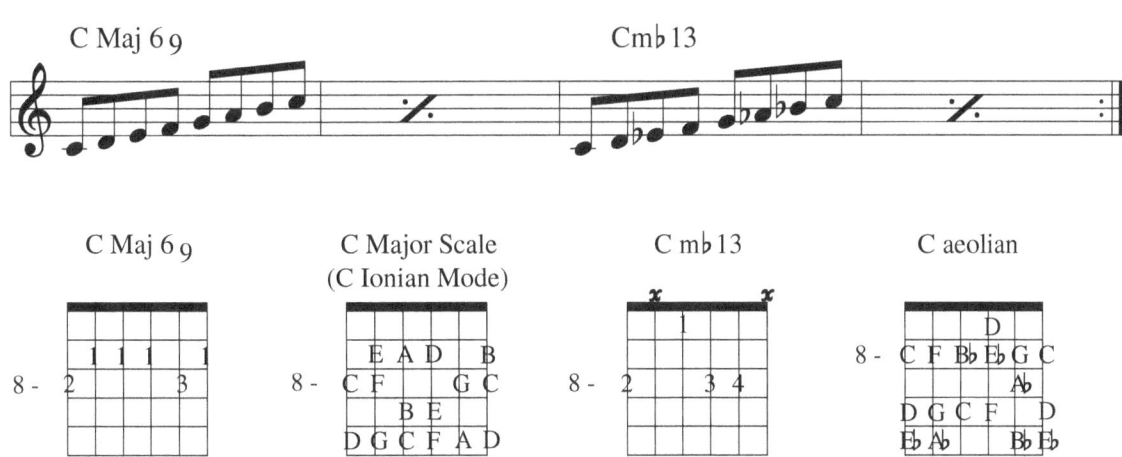

Major Chords a Minor 3rd Apart

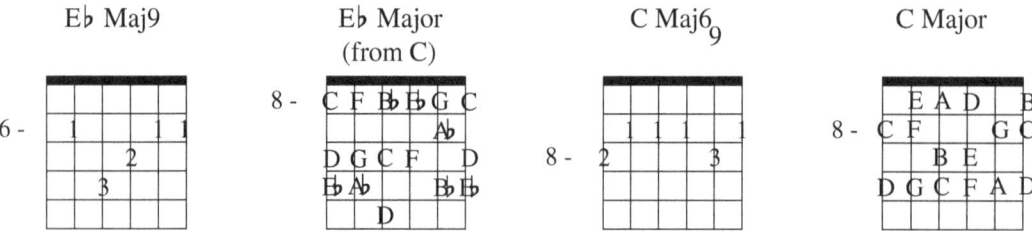

Dominant up a Whole Step to Major

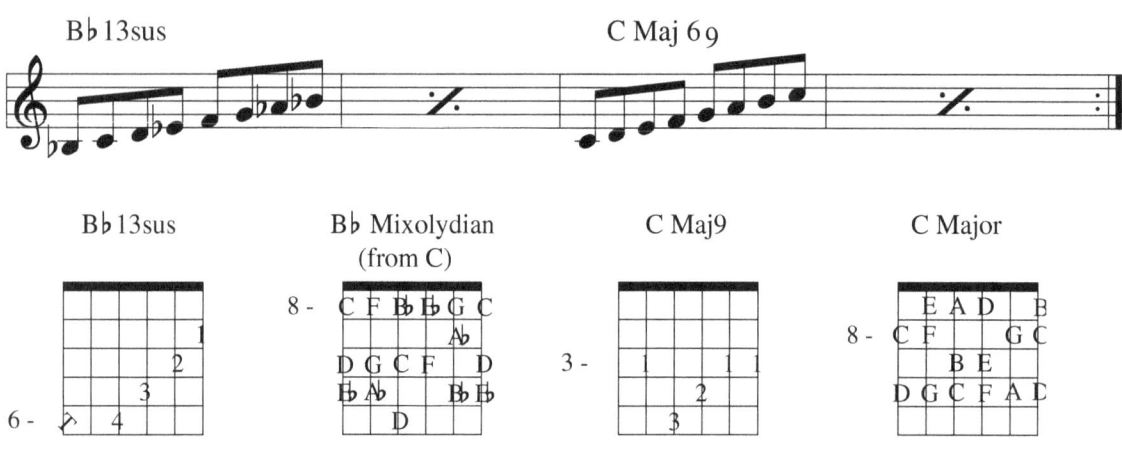

Major 7♯11 up a Major 3rd to Major

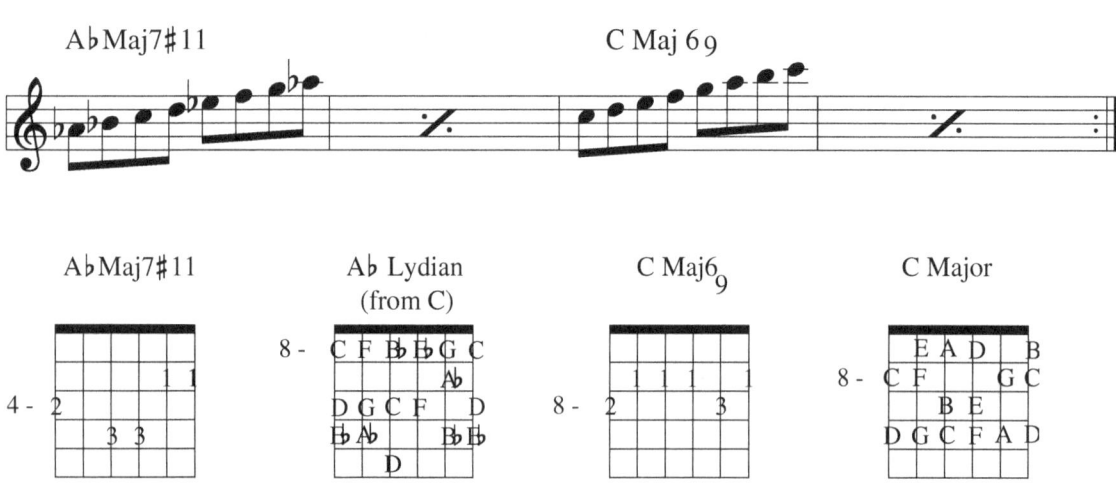

Appendix 1

Interval Exercises in 2nd Position

The G Major Scale in 3rds

Exercise 1 in 2nd Position

Exercise 2 in 2nd Position

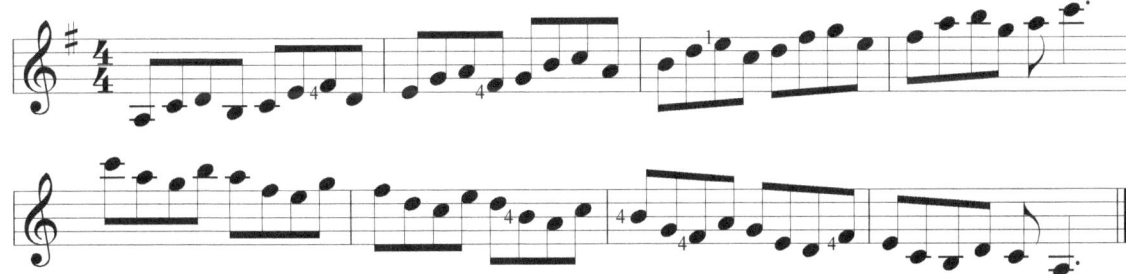

The G Major Scale in 4ths

Exercise 1 in 2nd Position

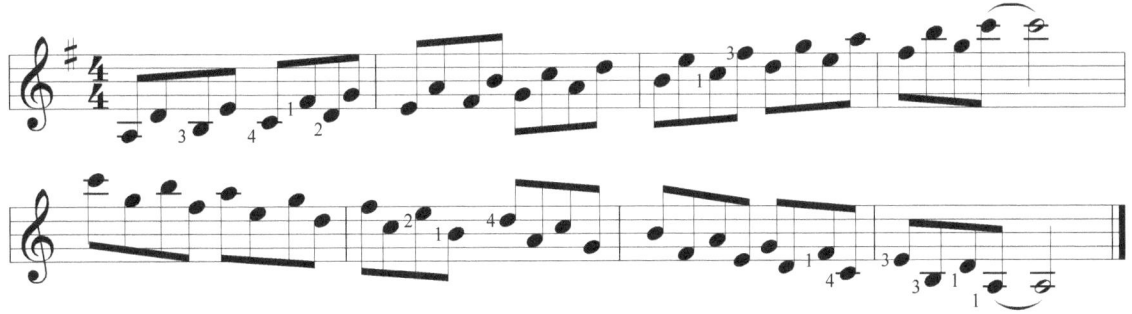

Exercise 2 in 2nd Position

The G Major Scale in 5ths

Exercise 1 in 2nd Position

Exercise 2 in 2nd Position

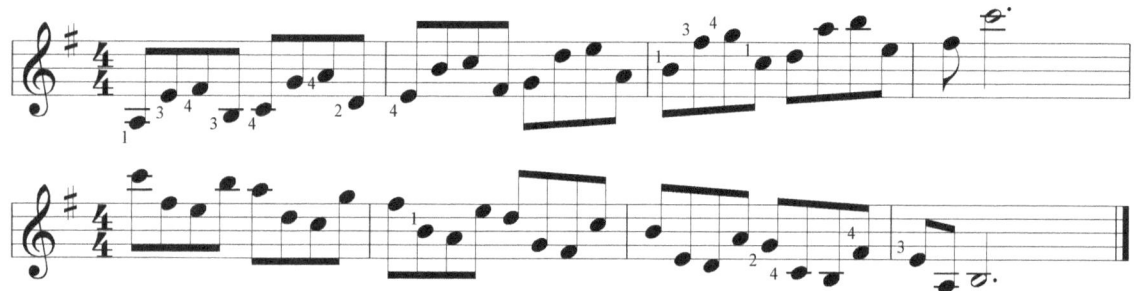

The G Major Scale in 6ths

Exercise 1 in 2nd Position

12 Major Scales in 2nd Position

The following exercise takes you through the major scales in 2nd position in all keys. With each key, be able to sing the root as you play. Practice these slowly at first, focusing on visualizing the note names on the neck as you play.

C Major

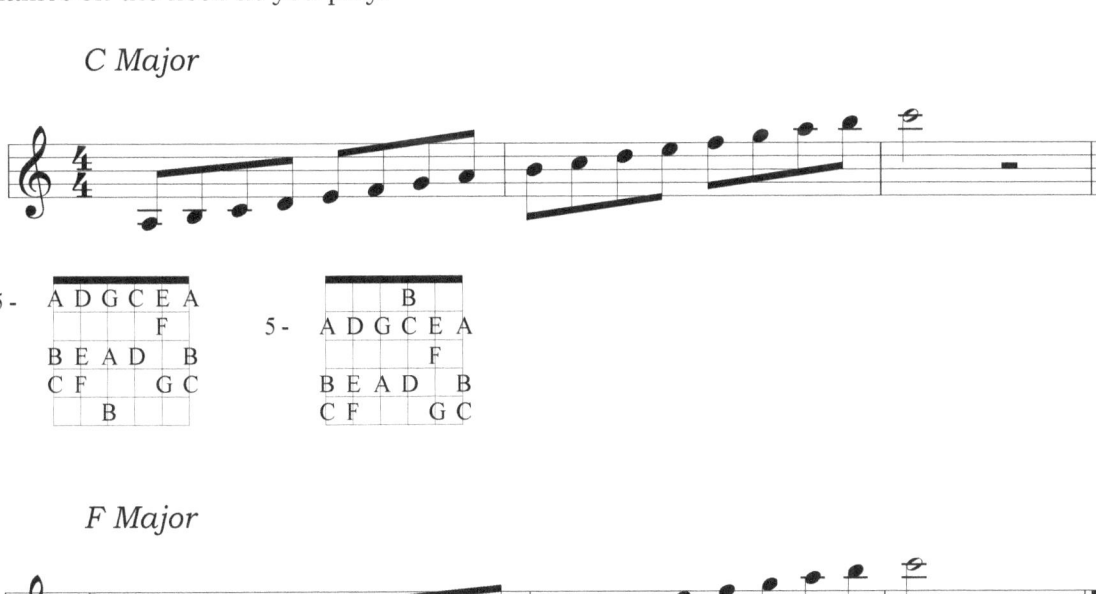

F Major

B♭ Major

E♭ Major

A♭ Major

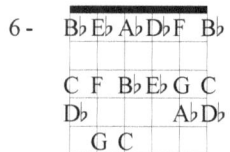
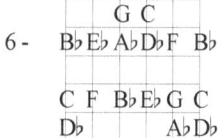

D♭ Major

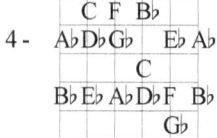

G♭ Major

F♯ Major

B Major

E Major

A Major

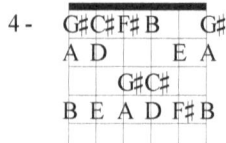

D Major

G Major

Exercise 1

Now play through these 2-octave major scales in all keys, up one and down the next. Focus on thinking the note names in each scale and visualizing them on the neck as you play.

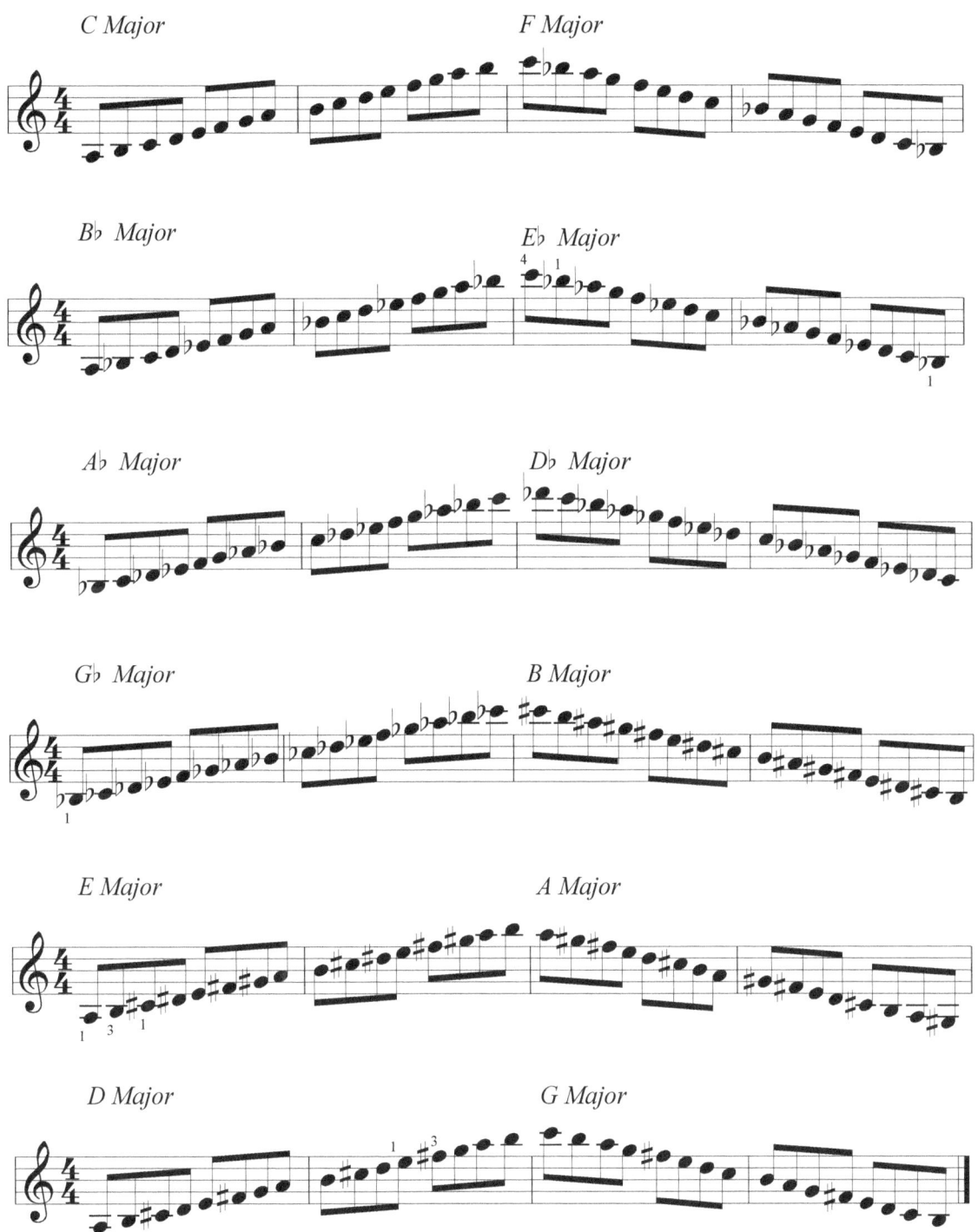

Appendix 2

12 Major Scales in 3rd Position

The following exercise takes you through the major scales in 3rd position in all keys. With each key, be able to sing the root as you play. Practice these slowly at first, focusing on visualizing the note names on the neck as you play.

C Major

F Major

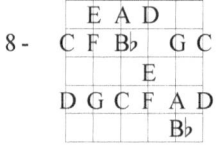

B♭ Major

   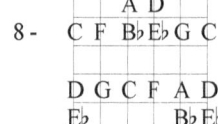

E♭ Major

A♭ Major

D♭ Major

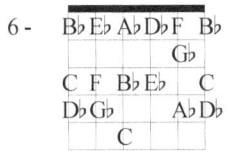 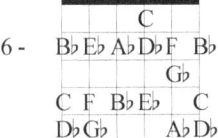

G♭ Major

F# Major

B Major

E Major

A Major

D Major

G Major

Appendix 3

12 Major Scales in 4th Position

The following exercise takes you through the major scales in 4th position in all keys. With each key, be able to sing the root as you play. Practice these slowly at first, focusing on visualizing the note names on the neck as you play.

C Major

F Major

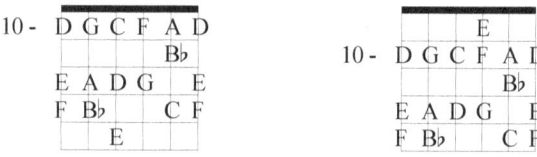

B♭ Major

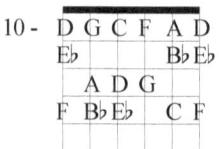

E♭ Major

A♭ Major

D♭ Major

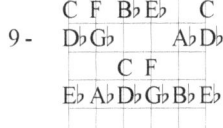

G♭ Major

F♯ Major

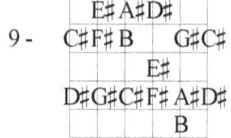

B Major

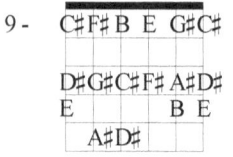 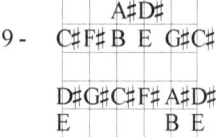

E Major

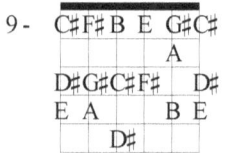 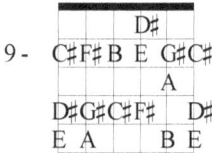

A Major

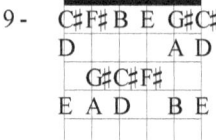

D Major

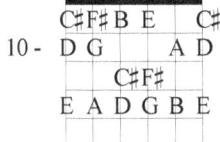

G Major

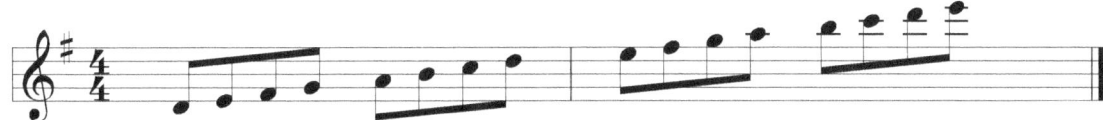

Appendix 4

12 Major Scales in 5th Position

The following exercise takes you through the major scales in 5th position in all keys. With each key, be able to sing the root as you play. Practice these slowly at first, focusing on visualizing the note names on the neck as you play.

C Major

F Major

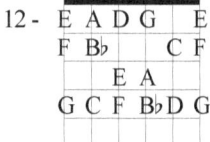

64

B♭ Major

E♭ Major

A♭ Major

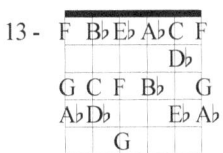
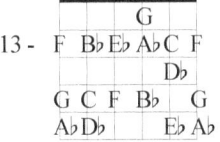

D♭ Major

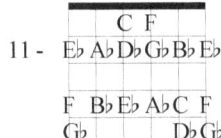

G♭ Major

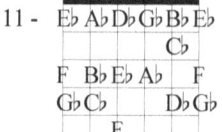
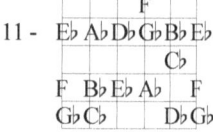

F# Major

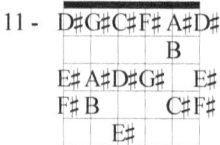
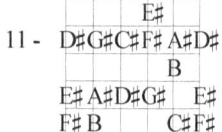

B Major

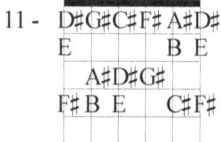

E Major

A Major

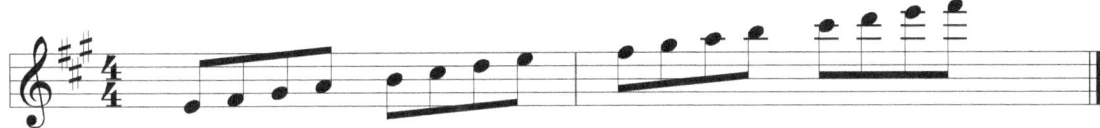

D Major

G Major

 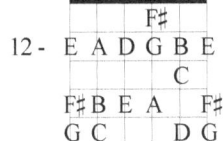